Author:
Ian Graham studied applied physics at City University in London, England. He then received a postgraduate degree in journalism, specializing in science and technology. Since becoming a freelance author and journalist, he has written more than one hundred children's nonfiction books.

Artist:
David Antram was born in Brighton, England, in 1958. He studied at Eastbourne College of Art and then worked in advertising for 15 years before becoming a full-time artist. He has illustrated many children's nonfiction books.

Series creator:
David Salariya was born in Dundee, Scotland. He has illustrated a wide range of books and has created and designed many new series for publishers in the UK and overseas. David established The Salariya Book Company in 1989. He lives in Brighton with his wife, illustrator Shirley Willis, and their son, Jonathan.

Editor: **Jamie Pitman**

Editorial Assistant: **Mark Williams**

© The Salariya Book Company Ltd MMIX
No part of this publication may be reproduced in whole or in part, or stored in a retrieval system, or transmitted in any form or by any means, electronic, mechanical, photocopying, recording, or otherwise, without written permission of the publisher. For information regarding permission, write to the copyright holder.

Published in Great Britain in 2009 by
The Salariya Book Company Ltd
25 Marlborough Place, Brighton BN1 1UB

ISBN-13: 978-0-531-21326-1 (lib. bdg.)   978-0-531-20517-4 (pbk.)
ISBN-10: 0-531-21326-9 (lib. bdg.)   0-531-20517-7 (pbk.)

All rights reserved.
Published in 2010 in the United States
by Franklin Watts
An imprint of Scholastic Inc.
Published simultaneously in Canada.

A CIP catalog record for this book is available
from the Library of Congress.

Printed and bound in China.
Printed on paper from sustainable sources.

PAPER FROM
SUSTAINABLE
FORESTS

You Wouldn't Want to Be a World War II Pilot!

Written by
Ian Graham

Illustrated by
David Antram

Created and designed by
David Salariya

Air Battles You Might Not Survive

Franklin Watts®
An Imprint of Scholastic Inc.
NEW YORK   TORONTO   LONDON   AUCKLAND   SYDNEY
MEXICO CITY   NEW DELHI   HONG KONG
DANBURY, CONNECTICUT

Contents

Introduction

You are 16. Home is San Antonio, Texas. The year is 1934. You're crazy about aircraft and flying. Your room is filled with models and posters of airplanes. You go to your local airfield, Stinson Field, to study pilots and their planes at every opportunity. The airfield's name recently changed to Windburn Field, but everybody still calls it Stinson Field.

The pilots there tell you about Charles Lindbergh. He was the first person to make a solo, nonstop flight across the Atlantic Ocean. Before he became world famous, he did his military flight training in San Antonio and kept a plane of his own at Stinson Field.

Watching the planes pitch and swoop through the sky, you realize that flying a plane is very tricky, and that proper training is crucial to develop the skills you'll need to survive. Who knows? In a few years, you may really need to know how to keep your plane in the sky!

YOU GET A JOB at the airfield cleaning small private planes and helping the mechanics. You hang out with the pilots and talk to them about flying. One way or another, you're going to be a pilot too.

You call it hard work...I call it research!

5

Learning to Fly

You are paid for your work with flying lessons. Experienced pilots teach you how to hold a plane level in the air, how to turn, and eventually how to take off and land. After you receive your pilot's license, you get a job flying a crop duster, dropping pesticides on local farms. You use the money to buy an old biplane of your own.

On weekends, you fly the biplane at air fairs. People flock to see pilots perform stunts with their planes. A favorite with the crowds is wing-walking. While you fly your plane, a friend stands on the top wing and waves to the crowd below. It's a spectacular but very risky trick.

Flying Solo

EVERY STUDENT PILOT has to make a successful flight alone before being awarded a pilot's license. It's called "going solo." You go solo a week after your 17th birthday.

I'm a true fly boy now!*

*slang for "pilot"

Air Shows

Aaaargh!

STUNT FLYING at air fairs in fragile 1930s planes can be very dangerous. A pilot can find himself hurtling toward the ground if a stunt goes wrong.

AIR RACES are popular in the 1930s. Crowds of spectators watch the planes race each other around a course marked by towers called pylons.

YOU GIVE FLYING LESSONS and take people on sightseeing flights to help pay for your plane. People are very eager to get a taste of flying.

6

7

Joining Up

In the 1930s, the newspapers are full of stories about the coming war in Europe. In 1933, Adolf Hitler's sinister Nazi party comes to power in Germany. Then in 1939, Nazi Germany invades Poland. As a result, Britain and France declare war on Germany. World War II, the long, bitter war between the Axis powers and the Allied nations,* has begun.

You learn that the British Royal Air Force (RAF) is recruiting American pilots. The thought of flying fantastic modern fighters like the Hurricane and Spitfire—while helping the British fight the Nazis—is very exciting. You apply to join the RAF, eager to start your training.

*The Axis powers included Germany, Japan, Italy, and several other countries. Great Britain, France, and Poland were among the major Allied nations at the start of the war. In 1941, the U.S. and the Soviet Union joined the Allies.

KA-BOOM!!

THE RAF ISN'T LOOKING for just any old pilot. You have to be able to say "yes" to a list of requirements:
• Are you between 20 and 31 years old?
• Do you have a pilot's license?
• Do you have 300 flying hours?
• Do you have good eyesight?
You don't need any military experience. That's a relief!

Handy Hint

Pay attention in class, or you'll never be a fighter pilot.

PILOTS HAVE TO LEARN Morse code. That's a way of sending messages as a stream of short bleeps (dots) and long bleeps (dashes). Each letter of the alphabet is made up of a different set of dots and dashes.

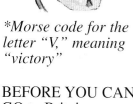

Dot-dot-dot-dash*

*Morse code for the letter "V," meaning "victory"

Sob!

BEFORE YOU CAN GO to Britain, you must complete an RAF training course in the United States. You wave one last good-bye to your family and set off for the nearest training center.

Training

IT'S BEEN QUITE A WHILE since you were in school, and you struggle to keep up with some of the classes.

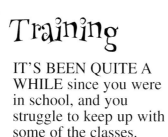

Piece of cake!

YOU DO YOUR FLIGHT TRAINING in a Stearman PT-17 biplane. It handles like your own biplane, so it's easy to learn how to fly it. Most pilots go solo within 12 hours.

Language Barrier

YOU CAN'T UNDERSTAND what your officers and mechanics are saying in their strange-sounding British accents.

Belt up!

*Are you a sprog,** old chum?*

*Be quiet!

**a pilot fresh from training

YOUR TEXAN DRAWL sounds just like a foreign language to British ears.

Howdy y'all!

?

Fighter Training

You arrive in Britain after a nerve-racking voyage across the Atlantic Ocean. As the passengers know very well, ships are at constant risk of attack by German submarines called U-boats. You begin to realize how much danger you are in. In London, you sign the official papers that make you an RAF officer and receive your uniform.

Your next stop is an Operational Training Unit (OTU), where you will be trained to fly a fighter. You meet Polish pilots who have also come to aid Britain's war effort. The Poles form a Polish Air Force in Britain and fight courageously alongside the RAF.

Tight Squeeze!

THE SPITFIRE'S COCKPIT is so cramped that the pilot needs help to get strapped in. Mechanics help the pilot and then give the windshield a final wipe before takeoff.

GUNNERY PRACTICE involves firing your guns at a windsock (called a drogue) that's towed behind another plane.

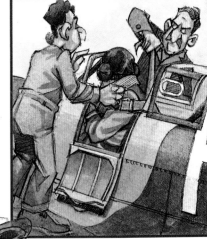

DW O K

RAT-A-TAT!

Leather helmet

Oxygen mask

Earphones

Life jacket
(called a "Mae West" after a film star of the same name)

Leather gloves

Parachute

Sheepskin-lined boots

Handy Hint

Keep an eye on your altitude gauge!

SNIP!

Looking good, huh?

Censored

YOUR LETTERS HOME arrive with holes in them because an official called a censor cuts out anything that he thinks might be useful to the enemy.

SNIP!

The Spitfire

R. J. Mitchell

THE SPITFIRE was designed by R. J. Mitchell, the leading British aircraft designer of the 1930s. Sadly, Mitchell never saw its success because he died in 1937 when he was only 42.

The Spitfire is the leading British fighter at the beginning of World War II. It's a small, fast, and heavily armed plane. Its main job is to attack enemy aircraft and protect Allied bombers from enemy fighters. It can also strike at targets on the ground. The Spitfire proves to be such a good all-around aircraft that it is built in greater numbers than any other Allied fighter.

Propeller

Whatta beauty!

SPITFIRE Mk Vb*

Engine: 1,440 horsepower Rolls-Royce Merlin
Length: 29 ft., 10 in. (9.1 m)
Wingspan: 36 ft., 10 in. (11.2 m)
Top speed: 375 mph (603 kmh)
Weapons: two 20mm cannons and four Browning machine guns
Maximum altitude: 37,000 ft. (11,277 m)
Manufacturer: Supermarine Aviation Works

Wing cannon

Landing gear

*pronounced "Mark Five B"

The Spitfire does not stay the same all through the war. There will be more than 20 different types of Spitfires, with different wings, guns, engines, and propellers. There is a naval version, too, called the Seafire.

THE SPITFIRE'S COCKPIT (left) is just big enough for the pilot to squeeze into. The canopy (below) slides back to make more room for the pilot to climb into the cockpit.

Handy Hint

Wear a silk scarf to keep your flying suit

from rubbing your neck raw.

BELTS OF AMMUNITION are loaded into the guns from underneath the wings.

Radio antenna

THE GROUND CREW swarms all over a Spitfire as soon as it lands. They refuel it and re-arm it for the next mission.

All-metal fuselage

Tail wheel

First Post

Xou arrive at an air base to join your fighter squadron. It's one of three RAF squadrons of American pilots, called Eagle Squadrons. You are replacing a pilot who was KIA*—a young American just like yourself. It's yet another reminder of the dangers you face.

For every pilot, there are up to ten men and women working on the ground to keep the planes repaired and ready for action. Each plane has its own crew chief and assistant. Together they look after the plane, giving work to other members of the ground crew when necessary.

WHEN YOU'RE ON cockpit alert, you have to sit in your plane for two hours, ready to go in case of an attack. If you see a bright flare bursting in the sky above you, you'd better scramble** because enemy aircraft are about to arrive.

*killed in action
**take off as quickly as possible

14

SMALL SWASTIKAS (Nazi symbols) are sometimes painted on the side of a plane to show how many enemy aircraft the pilot has shot down. Each swastika represents one aircraft.

KAY

Wheeeeeeee!

There may be trouble ahead...

KA-POW!

Listen up! I'm only going to say this once...

Major Tom? Come in, Major Tom!

BEFORE EACH PLANNED MISSION, all the pilots who will take part attend a briefing to learn the details.

GROUND CONTROLLERS plot the positions of Allied planes and Axis planes on a map. They talk with the Allied pilots by radio.

Combat

It isn't long before you get your first taste of combat. It's exciting, but the odds aren't great. A new fighter pilot in World War II has only a 50/50 chance of surviving his first five combat missions. Your first mission is to escort B-17 bombers attacking a factory in Germany. During the briefing, you begin to feel nervous. All the training is over and it's for real now. Lives will depend on what you do. The B-17 bombers have their own guns and gunners, but they can't maneuver quickly, which makes them easy targets for enemy fighters. You take off and join the bombers. On the way across the North Sea, you spot enemy fighters coming toward you!

Women at War

WHEN PLANES ARE LOST in combat, new planes are delivered by ferry pilots, many of whom are women.

PLANES OFTEN RETURN with battle damage. There might be bullet holes or part of a wing shot away. The ground crew has to repair the damage as fast as possible.

I hope this one lasts a bit longer!

THE SOVIET UNION has regiments of women pilots. Pilots in the 588th Night Bomber Regiment are known as the Night Witches.

The Night Witches fly old-fashioned Polikarpov Po-2 biplanes. They are slow, but they can turn quickly to escape an attack from an enemy fighter.

Allied and German fighters chase each other through the sky, twisting and turning to try to get each other's planes in their gun sights without leaving themselves exposed to enemy fire. Bursts of gunfire tear through the air.

The German fighters, out of ammunition, disappear as quickly as they arrived. You are relieved to have survived your first combat mission, but afterward you realize how terrifying it was.

Handy Hint

Keep looking around— enemy fighters can come from any direction.

Spitfire

B-17 bombers

Bandit* at two o'clock!

German FW-190 fighter

*enemy fighter

RUMBLE!

17

Passing Time

Fighter pilots don't fly all day, every day, even in wartime. Sometimes they have time off. Or they may be on standby, waiting for the signal to dash to their planes and take off. They also have to wait around if the weather is bad, if planes are out of service, or if the airfield is closed for repairs after an air raid.

Pilots pass the time reading, writing letters home, or playing games. If they're lucky, they get weekend leave—permission to be off duty all weekend! Off-duty pilots in southern England head for London.

Off Duty in London

Put that light out!

CITIES IN THE U.S. are brightly lit at night, but in London and other British cities, there's a blackout. No one is allowed to show any light at all. That way, German pilots won't know where to drop their bombs. People have to cover their windows with thick curtains to make sure that no light leaks outside. If any light gets out, you're in trouble!

AIR-RAID PRECAUTIONS (ARP) wardens patrol the streets and make sure that no one shows any light at night.

WATCHING A FILM or a stage show is a favorite night out in London, but be prepared for it to be spoiled by an air raid.

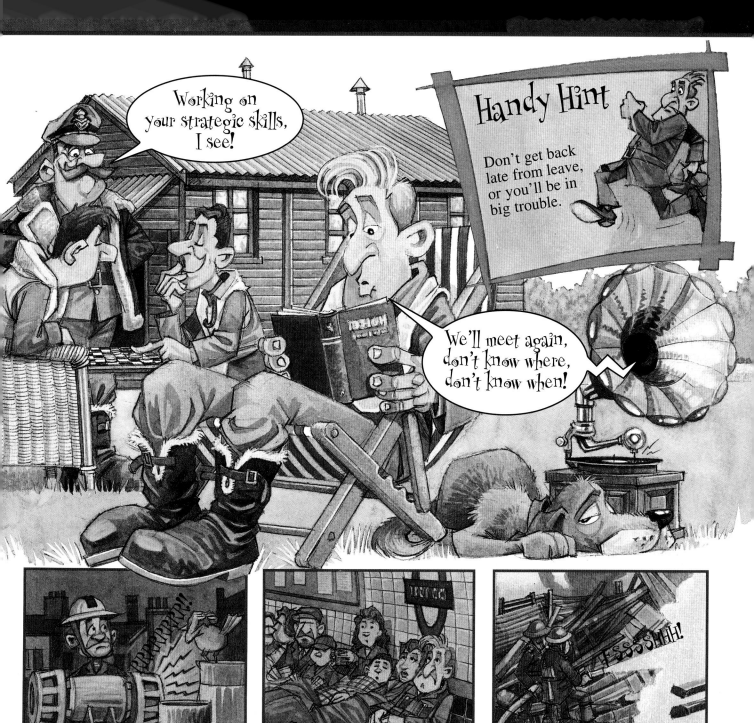

THE WAILING SOUND of air-raid sirens warns everyone that enemy bombers are on the way and bombs will start falling soon.

LONDONERS WAIT OUT the bombing in private air-raid shelters, public shelters, or underground subway stations.

WHEN PEOPLE EMERGE from the shelters after an air raid, some find that their homes are now just piles of rubble.

19

Bailing Out

You wear a parachute, but it's not on your back. You sit on it! The parachute and a life raft double as a seat cushion. You hope you'll never need them.

One day, you are taken by surprise by a Messerschmitt Bf-109. The 109 is the leading German fighter—and you're in its gun sights! As its pilot opens fire, bullets slam into the armor plate behind your head and shatter the cockpit canopy. Oil sprays out of bullet holes in your engine. You'll have to bail out!

YOU PUT ON YOUR PARACHUTE, slide the shattered canopy back, and climb out of the cockpit into the cold air outside.

SHATTER!!

Aaaargh! I'm done for!

Messerschmitt Bf-109

RAT-A-TAT!!

AS YOU TUMBLE THROUGH THE AIR, you pull the rip-cord handle, and your parachute billows open above you.

Phew!

Handy Hint

Remember how you were taught to roll when you land by parachute.

SPLISH!!

Survival

IF YOU LAND IN THE SEA, your life raft will keep you afloat while you wait for a ship to pick you up.

I hope I don't get bounced...*

IF YOU HAVE TO WAIT to be picked up, or if you land behind enemy lines, you'll need your survival kit. It contains maps, money, a knife, matches, and a compass.

*attacked by surprise

Pearl Harbor

On December 7, 1941, Japanese forces launch a surprise attack on the U.S. Pacific Fleet at Pearl Harbor, Hawai'i. More than 350 Japanese fighters, bombers, and torpedo planes attack in two waves. Five midget submarines join the attack.

Americans, who have not suffered a major attack on their home territory in living memory, are shocked. The next day, the United States declares war on Japan. Germany and Italy respond by declaring war on the United States. Now the United States will join the war in Europe as well as the war in the Pacific.

U.S. PRESIDENT FRANKLIN D. ROOSEVELT gives one of the most famous speeches of the 20th century on the day after the attack.

SOME AMERICAN PILOTS in the RAF ask the U.S. Embassy to transfer them to U.S. forces. They will get their wish, but not for another year.

AMERICAN FAMILIES hear their president describe the attack on the radio. The speech clearly signaled America's entrance into the war.

23

Pacific Fighters

Some of your friends became pilots in the U.S. Navy. Now they are fighting the Japanese in the Pacific. Navy pilots are based on flat-decked warships called aircraft carriers. The pilots have to take off from, and land on, a heaving deck that looks the size of a postage stamp from the air. If they miss their ship, they're swimming home!

The most successful U.S. Navy fighter is the Grumman F6F-5 Hellcat. The leading Japanese navy fighter is the Mitsubishi A6M2. The Allies call it the Zero.

BOOM!

Japanese A6M2 Zero fighter

The fighters took off at precisely 0800* hours...

SHORT NEWS FILMS called newsreels keep you informed about the Pacific war. They are shown in movie theaters before the feature films.

*8 a.m.: pronounced "oh-eight-hundred"

GRUMMAN F6F-5 HELLCAT (USA)

Engine: 2,000 horsepower Pratt & Whitney R-2800-10W
Wingspan: 42 ft., 10 in. (13.1 m)
Top speed: 380 mph (610 kmh)
Weapons: a variety of cannons, machine guns, rockets, bombs, and torpedoes
Maximum altitude: 37,300 ft. (11,370 m)

AS THE ALLIES ADVANCE across the Pacific, Japan uses a terrifying method of attack as a desperate last resort—kamikaze. Kamikaze pilots deliberately crash their planes onto Allied warships.

MITSUBISHI A6M2 ZERO (Japan)

Engine: 950 horsepower Nakajima Sakae 12
Wingspan: 39 ft., 4 in. (12 m)
Top speed: 331 mph (533 kmh)
Weapons: two 20mm cannons, two machine guns, and two bombs
Maximum altitude: 33,790 ft. (10,300 m)

Handy Hint

Watch your fuel gauge—you don't want to run out of fuel over the sea!

BLAM!!

Come on, give 'em more ack-ack!*

Only if you ack politely!

*anti-aircraft fire

25

Under U.S. Command

In September 1942, the RAF's Eagle Squadrons, manned by U.S. pilots, are transferred to the U.S. Army Air Forces (USAAF). They become the 4th Fighter Group of the 8th Air Force. All the pilots hand back their blue RAF uniforms and get olive USAAF uniforms. They continue to fly Spitfires until American Thunderbolt fighters arrive.

NOW THAT YOU'RE UNDER U.S. COMMAND, you get U.S. rations. It's great to eat pancakes, burgers, and cookies again.

Flying in a Steel Jug

THE P-47D THUNDERBOLT is known by its pilots as the "Jug." Jug is short for "Juggernaut"—meaning an unstoppable force—because the Thunderbolt is such a big, heavy, and powerful aircraft. It is the biggest single-seat fighter of its day.

26

IT'S A SAD DAY when your Spitfire is taken back by the RAF because you'll no longer get to fly in one.

*So long, old friend... *sniff**

Handy Hint

Don't fire too soon—wait until your target is within the range of your guns.

P-47D Thunderbolt

P-47D THUNDERBOLT

Engine: 2,535 horsepower Pratt & Whitney R-2800
Wingspan: 40 ft., 9 in. (12.4 m)
Top speed: 433 mph (697 kmh)
Weapons: eight Browning machine guns and two bombs or ten rockets
Maximum altitude: 42,000 ft. (12,800 m)

It's "plane" to see she's quite a fighter!

Congratulations, old boy!

ON YOUR LAST DAY under British command, you receive a medal to mark your service in one of the RAF's famous Eagle Squadrons.

Peace at Last

Germany surrenders on May 7, 1945. The war in Europe is over, though the war in the Pacific will continue for another three months. You are on leave in London when you hear the good news. You've survived, and soon it will be time to go home to the U.S.A.! You join thousands upon thousands of people in front of Buckingham Palace, the official home of the British royal family. When the royal family and Prime Minister Winston Churchill come out onto the palace's balcony, the crowd goes wild. Soldiers, sailors, and airmen throw their hats into the air. One woman, a Wren (a member of the Women's Royal Naval Service) named Kitty Cardle, loses her hat. When she goes on duty without it the next day, her superiors charge her with being improperly dressed!*

Hats off to the Allies!

Hurrah!

*The Wren, Kitty Cardle, is the author's mother.

Handy Hint

Wear your medals with pride—you've earned them.

YOU'RE DELIGHTED to be home, but you'll never forget the pilots who didn't make it back with you.

I sure won't miss the brussels sprouts!

ONE OF THE FIRST THINGS you do is have a meal—steak and french fries, and as much as you can eat. You're lucky, because food is still scarce back in Britain.

AT THE AIRFIELD where you learned to fly a biplane, a youngster admires your medals...

I'd like to be a pilot one day.

29

Glossary

Air fair A day or more of flying displays and competitions to entertain spectators.

Allies The countries that joined forces during World War II to fight against Germany, Italy, and Japan, which were known as the Axis powers.

Altitude Height above sea level.

Biplane A plane with two main wings, one above the other.

Briefing A meeting held before a mission to give pilots their instructions.

Canopy The transparent cover over a plane's cockpit.

Cockpit The part of a plane where the pilot sits.

Drogue A small parachute or windsock towed behind a plane and used as a practice target by fighter pilots.

Eagle Squadrons The three squadrons of American pilots in the RAF.

Ferry pilots Pilots who delivered new planes to RAF squadrons during World War II.

Fuselage The main body of an aircraft.

Going solo Flying a plane alone, without an instructor, for the first time.

Ground controllers A team of people who communicate with aircraft and keep track of their positions.

Ground crew The people who repair fighters and bombers, and keep them flying.

Gunnery practice Learning to use guns.

Kamikaze A Japanese word meaning "divine wind." It was the name for suicide attacks on Allied warships by Japanese pilots toward the end of the war.

Landing gear The wheels that support a plane while it is on the ground.

Mission A military operation such as an air attack or bombing raid. A mission or attack by one aircraft is also called a *sortie*.

Morse code A method of sending messages as a series of long and short sounds or visual marks.

Nazi Party The political party that ruled Germany from 1933 to 1945; led by dictator Adolf Hitler, it tried to exterminate certain ethnic groups, especially Jews.

Newsreel A short film showing events in the news.

Night Witches A regiment of all-women pilots in the Soviet Air Forces during World War II.

Pesticides Chemicals which are sprayed on crops to eliminate pests.

Pylon One of the towers that mark out the course for an air race.

RAF The British Royal Air Force.

Rip cord The cord that, when pulled, releases a parachute.

Scramble To get a plane into the air as quickly as possible.

Stunt An aerobatic maneuver made by a pilot to impress or entertain spectators.

U-boat The English term for a German submarine.

Wingspan The width of a plane from one wingtip to the other.

Wren A member of the Women's Royal Naval Service—the female branch of the British Royal Navy.

Index